Michael Jackson

Mike Wilson

SP
5/6

Published in association with The Basic Skills Agency

Hodder & Stoughton

Acknowledgements

Photos: pp. 16 (bottom), 22, 30, 36 and 43 © London Features.
  pp. 3, 7, 12, 16 (top and middle) and 40 © Redferns.
Cover photo: © Redferns.

Orders: please contact Bookpoint Ltd, 39 Milton Park, Abingdon, Oxon OX14 4TD. Telephone: (44) 01235 400414, Fax: (44) 01235 400454. Lines are open from 9.00–6.00, Monday to Saturday, with a 24 hour message answering service. Email address: orders@bookpoint.co.uk

British Library Cataloguing in Publication Data
Wilson, Mike
   Michael Jackson. – (Real lives) (Livewire)
   1. Jackson, Michael, 1958–   2. Rock musicians – United States –
   Biography   3. Readers
   I. Title
   782.4'2166'092

ISBN 0 340 70117 X

First published 1997
Impression number 10 9 8 7 6 5 4
Year 2004 2003 2002 2001 2000

Typeset by Fakenham Photosetting Ltd, Fakenham, Norfolk.
Printed in Great Britain for Hodder & Stoughton Educational, a division of Hodder Headline Plc, 338 Euston Road, London NW1 3BH by Page Bros, Norwich.

Contents

1 The voice of an angel

The door of your dressing room opens
and your dad looks in.
'Come on boys,' he says.
'Time to go to work.'

You go with your brothers
out into the corridor.
You pass the dancers and the strippers.
You pass the other dressing rooms,
where your brothers watch the girls
get undressed.

Then you all run out onto the stage
and start your dance routine.
You've all worked so hard to get it perfect.

And when you start to sing,
everybody stops to look at you.

Your voice is the voice of an angel.
Or a superstar.

You win the talent contest easily.
You always do.

But there's no time to enjoy yourselves.
Your dad packs you all into the van
and you drive through the night,
back home.

You get two hours sleep,
then you have to get up and go to school.

Your name is Michael Jackson.
The year is 1964,
and you are just six years old.

You were born on August 29, 1958
in Gary, Indiana.

You have four brothers and three sisters.
You are the youngest boy.

Michael Jackson.

It's not a normal childhood,
but then you are not a normal child.
You're special.
Everybody says so, right from the start.

Your dad, Joe Jackson,
works hard in a steel factory.
He plays guitar in a band,
and he dreams that music
will be a way out
for him and the Jackson family.

Your dad makes you and your brothers
work so hard
to become the Jackson Five.
He wants his boys to make it to the very top.
Only the best is good enough,
so he shouts at you,
and frightens you,
so you'll work harder to get it right.

Sometimes he hits you,
but it's just because he wants you
to be perfect.

2 The Jackson Five

In 1967, you sign your first record deal,
with Tamla Motown.
You get to meet all the Motown stars,
including Diana Ross and the Supremes.

You are out on the road with your dad
all the time,
and you miss your mum.

Diana Ross is a world-famous superstar.
You move into her house for a while,
and she becomes your friend.
You fall in love with her a little.

You are ten years old.

The Motown boss, Berry Gordy, says
he will make the Jacksons into superstars.
He promises that your first three singles
will all go to Number 1.

But Berry Gordy was wrong.

In fact, the first four singles
all got to Number 1
in America in 1970.

The songs were
I Want You Back and *ABC*,
The Love You Save and *I'll Be There*.

The whole world goes crazy
for the Jackson Five.

Girls come and camp outside your house.
One girl gets inside the house,
and you find her waiting for you
in the bath.

The Jackson Five.

At first, the fans make you frightened.
You are still just a small boy.
But somehow you have to learn
to live with the pressure.

In 1971 and 1972
you start your solo career,
making singles without your brothers.
All these singles make it to the Top Ten.

They are
Got To Be There and *Rockin' Robin*,
I Wanna Be Where You Are,
Ain't No Sunshine and *Ben*.

Ben was the theme song from a film
about a boy with a pet rat.

But you are not happy
with the way your career is going.
You said,
'They wanted me to sing a certain way,
and I knew they were wrong . . .
This was in 1972 when I was 14 years old . . .'

Three years later, when you are 17,
you do a deal with CBS.
And the Jacksons split
from the Motown record label.

Motown boss Berry Gordy is furious.
Your dad,
who is still the Jacksons' manager,
is furious.

But you know you are doing the right thing.

Now you take on the job
of managing the Jacksons.

Your next big hits
come from the *Destiny* album,
released in 1978.

Songs like *Blame It On The Boogie*
and *Shake Your Body Down To The Ground*
proved you could still make hit singles.

You also proved you were a fantastic dancer!

By now you are 20.
You are growing older,
growing away from the rest of the family.
After *Destiny*, you want to make a solo album.

You want it to be
the biggest and best album of all time.

You hire the best producer,
and in 1979,
you release *Off The Wall*.
You are 21 years old.

Michael Jackson in 1979.

All the singles hit the Top Ten
in Britain and America.

The singles include
Don't Stop Till You Get Enough,
Rock With You,
and the slow, sad song
She's Out Of My Life.

The album is a top seller all over the world.
It sells six million copies in America alone,
and you make over $15 million.
But you know you can do better.

Ever since I was a little boy, you say later,
I had dreamed of creating
the biggest record of all time.

That record is *Thriller.*

3 A new image

Thriller takes nearly three years to make,
and costs three quarters of a million dollars.
Because you want it to be perfect.

Every little detail is planned carefully.
Songs are recorded over and over,
then thrown out, when you write better ones.
In all, you try nearly 300 songs.

Three of the songs that do make the album,
Billie Jean, *Thriller* and *Beat It*,
have fantastic videos to go with them.

The *Thriller* video is 14 minutes long.
It is the most expensive pop video ever made.
Even *The Making of Thriller*,
the video-about-the-video, is a best-seller.

MTV, the cable pop video channel,
does not often show videos by black artists.
But they cannot ignore Michael Jackson.
They show all your videos,
and this increases sales of the album.

Today, *Thriller* has sold
nearly 50 million copies.
It's the biggest-selling record ever.
It's made you over $200 million.

You designed every image
for your *Thriller* videos,
the stories, the sets, the clothes.
Your black clothes,
black shiny shoes, white socks,
became famous, your trade-mark.
You also designed all your own dances.

You even re-designed your own face.

Ever since you were a teenager,
you have worried about your looks.

You hated your skin, with its teenage spots,
and you hated the look of your nose.
People had teased you about it
when you were small.

'I got very shy,
and became embarrassed
to meet people,'
you say later.
'It messed up my whole personality.'

In the 1980s you start having plastic surgery.
You change the shape of your nose,
and your skin is lighter.
Some people say, you want to be white.

Or – you want to look more like Diana Ross.
Or – you want to stop looking like your father
and the other Jacksons.
You want to leave that life behind.

Michael before plastic surgery

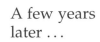A few years
later . . .

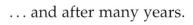. . . and after many years.

No, you tell us.
It's just make-up,
to hide a skin disease.

Some people say
you're trying to be a mystery,
to keep the public interested in you.

After your plastic surgery,
it's difficult to tell if you're young or old,
black or white, male or female.

It's all part of the Michael Jackson image.

You want to look special.

You want to be perfect.

4 'I was lonely'

Your favourite story is Peter Pan,
the story of a boy who never grows up.
Peter Pan lives in Neverland.
It starts with the words,

     Every child grows up – except one.

You see yourself as Peter Pan,
because you never grew up.
You never had the chance.

You were too busy,
singing and dancing in the Jackson Five,
to grow up like a normal boy.

I was lonely, you say.
I used to cry from loneliness.
I would look out
and see all the children playing,
and it would make me cry.

Your father made you work so hard,
he was more like your manager,
not your father.
'. . . I still don't know him', you write later,
'and that's sad,
for a son who hungers to know his father.'

Then your father had affairs,
and split up from your mother.

As soon as you're rich and famous,
you move away from the rest of your family.

You build your own Neverland,
and fill it with toys and pets and children.
They are easier to talk to than grown ups.
You say, 'Grown ups pretend they like you
when deep down inside they hate you . . .'

'I love children so much . . .
they don't know any prejudice . . .
and if they don't like you, they'll tell you.'

All your friends are children,
boys between 10 and 14 years of age.

You buy them presents and holidays,
and you take them everywhere with you.
They even come and live with you.

If the parents start to worry,
you buy them presents or give them money
to show them you are kind and loving.

One of your friends is Macauley Culkin,
star of the hit movies
Home Alone and *Home Alone 2*.

Like you, Macauley is a child star.

Many of the women in your life,
and the girlfriends you are seen with,
Liz Taylor, Tatum O'Neal, Brooke Shields,
were child stars, just like you.

One day you tell a journalist,
'I've never had an adult relationship.
I have never made love.
I don't want to just yet . . .'

Then you say,
'One of the worst memories . . .
is a stripper who played the same club we did
when I was six . . . It was disgusting.'

And you add,
'I just don't have the time
to have a steady girlfriend.
My career comes first.'

But then your career was almost ruined
by your love for young children.

Michael with his great friend, Liz Taylor.

5 Dream come true?

In August 1993,
you meet a man called Evan Chandler.
He is the father of Jordan Chandler,
a 13-year-old boy
who has been staying with you.

Evan Chandler says you abused his son.

You met Jordy and his mother, June,
a year ago, in May 1992.
It was pure luck. Your car broke down,
and June and Jordy came with the pick-up truck
to help get you home.

For 13-year-old Jordy,
it was a dream come true.
And for you it was a special meeting too.

Pretty soon you're phoning Jordy every day,
from all over the world.

You take Jordy, and his mother and sister
to Las Vegas,
and to Monte Carlo with you.
You take them home with you,
and they stay with you for a month.

You had never been so happy.
It was like you had found
a whole new family for yourself.

June didn't live with Jordy's father any more.
They were separated.
Now Evan, Jordy's father,
was saying you had abused the boy.

Jordy's lawyer said,
'Michael was in love with the boy.'
But then he added,
'It was a gentle, soft, caring,
warm, sweet relationship.'

It was innocent.
Nothing suspicious.

Then the police raid your house,
and your parents' house.
They take away boxes of papers and photos
from your bedroom.

Now you face two court cases.
One from Evan Chandler,
and one from the police.
The police are planning
four separate court cases
in four separate American cities.

You tell everyone you are innocent.
'There has never been any sexual abuse . . .
I could never hurt a child . . .'

The Jackson family
come forward to defend you.
'I raised my boy,
and I know he is innocent.'

Other young boys
come forward to defend you.
'Michael hugged me and kissed me,
but he did it
just like you would kiss your own mother,
or hug your own friend . . .
He's like your best friend, only big.'

'He sleeps on one side of the bed,
and I sleep on the other,
and it's a big bed.
We just go to sleep.'

But other stories come out too.
Other boys, parents,
people who used to work for you
all tell stories that make you look guilty.

Jordy's father says:
'You're going to be sorry, Michael . . .
I will get everything I want.
The mother is going to lose Jordan,
and Michael's career will be over . . .
I know Michael is bad for my son,
I know what he has to hide.'

6 Breakdown

You are on the other side of the world,
in the middle of a World Tour,
trying to thrill your fans
with the biggest and best live show ever.

The pressure is all too much.

You break down in Bangkok,
and have to cancel a show
for 40,000 waiting fans.

In the end,
the rest of the tour is cancelled.
News leaks out
that you are addicted to pain-killing drugs.
In a message to the press,
you tell us it all started seven months ago.

You were making a TV commercial for Pepsi.
A flash-bomb exploded near you
and set your hair on fire.

You were rushed to hospital, badly burned.
You needed more plastic surgery,
and you were given powerful painkillers
to get you through.

Then came the World Tour,
and Evan Chandler's allegations against you.
In a shaky voice, you tell us,

'The pressure from these false allegations . . .
coupled with the incredible energy
needed for me to perform . . .
left me physically and emotionally exhausted.
I became more and more dependent
on the painkillers
to get me through the tour.

It has become an addiction,
and I need treatment . . .'

You go into hiding for four weeks,
and get medical help.

Later, we find out that you stayed in England,
at a mansion owned by Elton John,
while you recovered
from your drug addiction.

When you get back home to America,
in December 1993,
the police still want to question you
about Jordy Chandler.

They examine your naked body,
to check Jordy's story.
'It was a nightmare,' you say,
'a horrifying nightmare.'

There are court cases everywhere.

In Santa Barbara,
a jury meets to hear Jordy's evidence.
They have to decide
whether to start a court case against you.

The promoters of your World Tour sue you.
They say you got paid for shows,
and then cancelled them,
and they want their money back.

A children's charity sues you for fraud.
They say you cheated them out of $150 million
for sales of Michael Jackson clothes
and watches.

There's even a court case against you
by two songwriters.
They accuse you
of stealing ideas for songs from them.

Then you start a court case of your own.
It's against your sister LaToya,
to stop her telling more stories
about your sex life.

Happier days – Michael with his sister, LaToya in the 1980s.

But the Jordan Chandler case
never gets to court.

In January 1994,
Jordan agrees not to speak against you.
Nobody knows
how much money you agree to pay Jordan.
Some say it's as much as $50 million.
The case against you is dropped.

You would pay all the money in the world
to keep your private life out of the courts.

But some people think
that making this deal is a bad move.

As your sister LaToya puts it,
'. . . it's a big mistake . . .
because it shows guilt,
because you're buying someone off.
Michael has done that a lot.
My family has done that a lot.'

A top lawyer
sums up what people are saying.
'If you have a lot of money,
you can buy your way out of trouble.'

Meanwhile, Pepsi-Cola drop you
from their $15 million advertising campaign.
Then the Disney Corporation stop your 3-D film,
Captain Eo
from playing at Euro-Disney.

You try to put it all behind you.
You work hard
on the children's charity you set up,
the Heal The World Foundation.
You set up special rooms for children
in top hospitals.
You send thousands of dollars
to the children of Bosnia.

You work hard on your next album, *HIStory*.
All your live shows and videos
show you with children,
protecting them, caring for them,
being adored by them.

7 Another dream come true?

And then you get married.

Lisa Marie Presley
is the daughter of Elvis Presley.
She is an only child.
When she reaches 30,
she will inherit $200 million.

Like you, she grew up in public.
Like you, she feels robbed of her childhood.
Like you, she is rich enough
to have anything she wants.

Lisa Marie first meets you when she is six,
when Elvis brings her to watch the Jackson Five.
You are ten years older.

You become friends,
and during the Jordan Chandler case
Lisa Marie sees you on television,
holding back the tears,
telling the world you are innocent . . .

and Lisa Marie falls in love.

On May 6, 1994,
Lisa Marie is divorced from her first husband.
Three weeks later, she marries you in secret,
in the Dominican Republic.

She says,
'I am very much in love with Michael.
I dedicate my life to being his wife.'

But you are separated only 18 months later,
in December 1995.

Lisa Marie wanted to be a singer,
just like her famous father.
She wanted you to help her start her career.
She wanted to use your fame
and your contacts in the music business.

But you were too busy with your own career,
producing your own album.
It was to be called
HIStory Past, Present and Future, Book 1.

But you still love Lisa Marie.
You still keep a photo of her
by your bed in Neverland.

Michael and Lisa Marie Presley in 1994.

8 'A bit of reality'

In 1983,
Thriller became the biggest selling album
of all time.
That's a hard act to follow,
and you never have the same success again.

Your next albums,
Bad (1987), *Dangerous* (1991)
and *HIStory* (1995)
are all best-sellers all over the world.
But . . . something is missing.

You change the clothes you wear.
After the black shoes and white socks of *Thriller*
comes black leather, silver studs,
straps and buckles,
and bullet belts for *Dangerous*.

Then comes gold braid, soldiers' uniforms,
for *HIStory*.
You look like a world leader, a dictator,
always bigger and grander than before.

Then in 1996,
you release your latest single, *Earth Song*,
and it's the Number 1 single all over the world.

In the *Earth Song* video,
you appear like Jesus Christ,
gathering all the children of the world
in your arms,
protecting them from the wind and the rain.
You make the dead trees and the dying earth
come back to life.

Some people begin to think
you're going a bit too far,
pretending to be the saviour of the world.

At the 1996 Brit Awards in London
Jarvis Cocker decides to tell you so.
He jumps on stage behind you.
He turns his back and waggles his bum at you.
People laugh. People clap and cheer.

One of your bodyguards is there with you.
He chases Jarvis from the stage.

Later you say you are
'sickened, saddened, shocked,
upset, cheated, angry . . .'

Michael performing *Earth Song*.

Jarvis Cocker is arrested for assault,
but no-one was assaulted, and no-one was hurt.
So Jarvis is soon freed.

Jarvis says,
'I've not got anything against Michael Jackson.
Anyone who invented the moonwalk
is all right by me.
It was that performance that was in bad taste.'

And Jarvis adds,
'I think it would be good for him
to get a bit of reality into his life.'
But Jarvis Cocker doesn't understand.
How can he?

You are Michael Jackson.
You have been a child star,
and a multi-millionaire,
since you were eight years old.

The one thing you can't have
is 'a bit of reality' in your life.

It's the one thing you can't buy.

And then, in November 1996,
you marry again.

Debbie Rowe is blonde, and white,
and a year younger than you.

You have known her for 15 years.
She is a nurse,
working for the L.A. doctor
who treated your skin problems.

You have two children with Debbie:
a boy called Prince Michael Joseph Jackson
and a girl called Paris Michael Katherine Jackson.

Prince Michael is two years old,
and Paris is one,
when Debbie files for divorce
in October 1999.

Right from the start,
rumours have been leaking out:

You are a very loving father.
You love to sing and dance for your kids.
But their mother is not always there.

Nurses and servants look after Prince and Paris.
They are not allowed to kiss them.

Spoons and bowls are all boiled
before they are used.
Right after,
they are all thrown away.

Any toys the children touch
are thrown away at the end of each day.

The rumours might be true.
Or they might not be true.
We will never know your side of the story.

Michael and his second wife Debbie Rowe.

The last word goes to one of your loyal fans.

Amanda Collinson is 18
and she lives in Essex.

When you were in London
for the Brit Awards,
Amanda waited all day outside your hotel.
She was hoping to get to see you,
or touch you.

She wasn't disappointed.

'He touched my finger!' she screamed.
'I can't believe it!
I love him so much,
it was the happiest moment of my life!'

You are Michael Jackson. You are not a god.
You are not the saviour of the world.

But to your fans, who love you,
that's not important.